Dick Whittington

Pippa Goodhart

Illustrated by
Nick Schon

OXFORD
UNIVERSITY PRESS

UNIVERSITY PRESS

Great Clarendon Street, Oxford, OX2 6DP,
United Kingdom

Oxford University Press is a department of the University of Oxford.
It furthers the University's objective of excellence in research, scholarship,
and education by publishing worldwide. Oxford is a registered trade mark of
Oxford University Press in the UK and in certain other countries

Text © Pippa Goodhart 2003

The moral rights of the author have been asserted

First published in this edition 2016

All rights reserved. No part of this publication may be reproduced, stored
in a retrieval system, or transmitted, in any form or by any means, without
the prior permission in writing of Oxford University Press, or as expressly
permitted by law, by licence or under terms agreed with the appropriate
reprographics rights organization. Enquiries concerning reproduction outside
the scope of the above should be sent to the Rights Department, Oxford
University Press, at the address above.

You must not circulate this work in any other form
and you must impose this same condition on any acquirer

British Library Cataloguing in Publication Data
Data available

978-0-19-837744-3

5 7 9 10 8 6 4

Paper used in the production of this book is a natural, recyclable product
made from wood grown in sustainable forests. The manufacturing process
conforms to the environmental regulations of the country of origin.

Printed in China by Leo Paper Products Ltd.

Acknowledgements
Cover and inside illustrations by Nick Schon
Inside cover notes written by Becca Heddle

Contents

1	Streets Paved with Gold	5
2	Little Puss	14
3	Nobody Can Stop You Dreaming	22
4	Quite Grand	31
5	A Venture	37
6	Turn Again	43
7	Pearls and Kittens	47
8	A Merchant Gentleman	56
	About the author	64

Chapter 1

Streets Paved with Gold

All day, every day, Dick stood and watched his master's pigs. And as he stood, he dreamed.

Dick dreamed of living in a place full of people and buildings, instead of pigs and trees.

One day, the squire's son came riding by. He looked down from his high horse and he asked Dick, "What are you staring at, Pig Boy? Have you never seen fine clothes from London before?"

"Please, sir, have you been to London?" asked Dick.

"Not yet," said the squire's son.
"But I shall go to London next year to become a fine gentleman. Did you know that the streets of London are paved with gold?"

"With gold?" said Dick. "Wow!"

That evening Dick knocked on his master's door.

"What is it?" asked the farmer.

"Er," said Dick. "I've come to tell you that I'm leaving. I'm going to London."

"To London?" said the farmer.

"Yes," answered Dick. "In London the streets are paved with gold."

"Indeed?" said the farmer with a smile. "Well, good luck to you, Dick. But remember that you can always come home if things don't work out as you hope."

The farmer gave Dick a few coins and his wife gave Dick some food to eat on his journey. Dick bundled his things into a cloth. Then he tied it on to his pig stick and set off.

After five days of walking, Dick came to the top of a hill and looked down on London at last.

"Oh, it *is* golden!" said Dick, because the sinking sun on the river made it look that way. "It's beautiful!"

Spires and turrets and sailing ship masts and flags spiked the sky within a great wall that hugged all around London.

Dick could hear church bells, their sounds all tumbling together. They seemed to be calling Dick to them.

Dick swung his stick over his shoulder and ran the rest of the way.

Dick went through a gateway into streets crowded with houses and people and smells and sounds that were strange to him.

He looked down at the ground under his feet. "It's just ordinary cobblestones!" he said.

"Well, what were you expecting?" asked a man.

"Gold," said Dick.

"Gold?" laughed the man. "I can see that you've not been to London before. But you've chosen a good day to come. Watch what happens in these streets tonight. You'll see a sight as fine as any street paved with gold!"

Chapter 2

Little Puss

The evening darkened. Bonfires and lanterns were lit. Then a grand and noisy procession began.

Dick pushed through to the front of the crowd to watch. There were archers and soldiers with breastplates glinting in the torchlight.

There were drummers and pipers.
Trumpeters on horseback blasted sounds
that Dick felt in his throat. He cheered
with the rest of the crowd.

Last of all came rows of boys in fine
cloaks. Dick pointed. "Please," he asked a
woman. "Who are they?"

"Those are the apprentice boys. They are learning a trade," she told him. "In a year or two, they will all be fine gentlemen."

"Like the squire's son," thought Dick. "And that's what I want to be! An apprentice."

"See that man there?" said the woman. She pointed to a man splendid in red and gold. "That's our Lord Mayor. He was an apprentice boy himself, once."

"Please, how can I become an apprentice boy and march with them?" asked Dick.

"You?" laughed the woman. "You can't. You're only a beggar boy."

In the days that followed, Dick earned a penny or two by helping to load and unload the ships.

He listened to the sailors talk about India, Africa and China. He saw the fine silver and rich silks, and smelled the wonderful spices and sweet perfumes that came from these faraway places.

"I'd like to be a merchant, trading English wool for all these wonderful things," thought Dick.

Each night, as he settled in to sleep beside the slap-slopping, salty, smelly river, Dick dreamed.

He dreamed of owning a big, beautiful ship and a warm home to come back to. Dreaming helped him forget the rats that scrabbled for scraps in the mud.

One night, a sudden squeaking made Dick sit up. He saw two rats fighting fiercely. But then he saw that one of them wasn't a rat, after all.

It was a little cat.

She was fighting a rat that was bigger than she was.

"Leave her alone!" shouted Dick.

The rat twisted around to bite the cat on the neck. But Dick picked up his stick and he whacked the rat away.

Then Dick picked up the cat. He knew how to care for animals.

"Hey, hey, little Puss," he soothed.

He stroked her until her trembling turned into purrs and they curled up to sleep together.

Chapter 3
Nobody Can Stop You Dreaming

The next morning, Dick woke nicely warm with the cat still on his chest. "Hello, Puss," he said. "Are you as hungry as I am?"

They went looking for food. The cat sniffed around the feet of the fish stall owners. But Dick dawdled, looking longingly at a pile of richly coloured silks and velvets.

"Do you like them?" asked the grand gentleman who stood by the stall. Dick nodded.

"Are you hungry?" asked the man.

"I am, sir," said Dick.

"Then you may go to my kitchen and tell Cook that I have sent you for a meal."

"Thank you, sir," said Dick with a bow.

Mr Hugh Fitzwarren's house was
very grand. Cook was big and loud,
clattering her pans in a kitchen
hot with smoke and steam.

She gave Dick a piece of pie and sent
him outside to the yard.

There were rats skittering among the
empty barrels, looking for scraps.

"Do you want some pie?" Dick asked Puss. But Puss was busy, prowling and pouncing around the barrels.

She soon caught a big brown rat.

"Clever Puss!" said Dick, and he gave her a piece of his pie.

A scuffle and squeak later, and Puss was back with a second rat.

"Good Puss!" said Dick.

Just then, Mr Fitzwarren strode into his yard.

Dick jumped up and bowed low. Puss paced forward with her nose up high and dropped a rat at the fine gentleman's feet.

Mr Fitzwarren bent down to Puss and rubbed her behind her ears.

He said to Dick, "Your little cat is quite a hunter. We have too many rats. Will you sell your cat to me?"

"No, sir," said Dick. "She's not for sale."

"In that case," said Mr Fitzwarren, "Would you and your cat *both* like to work for me? I will pay you."

"Oh, yes, please, sir!" said Dick.

So Dick and Puss were sent to work in the kitchen.

Cook shut Puss outside.

"You go and catch them rats," she said.

Dick worked in Mr Fitzwarren's kitchen for many months.

He scrubbed vegetables and he plucked the feathers off birds.

He turned the spit over the roasting fire. He emptied the slops and he swept the floor.

Dick had a warm place to sleep in a corner of the kitchen. He had his friend Puss and plenty to eat, but it was hard work.

And Dick still dreamed of having his own ships that would sail the seas and bring things from across the world.

Cook scolded Dick for his daydreaming. "You're a useless good-for-nothing, Dick Whittington! Stop thinking of what will never be. Fetch that pan and be quick about it!"

But nobody can stop a person from dreaming.

Chapter 4

Quite Grand

One cold day, Puss jumped on to a window sill and saw Miss Alice Fitzwarren sitting beside a fire.

Puss slipped into the room and Alice took Puss on to her knee. Alice became good friends with Puss, and with Dick too.

"I won't always be a kitchen boy," Dick told her. "I want to be a merchant like your father."

"Then you'd better learn to read and write," said Alice.

She taught Dick to read and write with a quill pen.

Cook was cross, of course. "Who do you think you are, Dick Whittington? Too high and mighty for honest kitchen work, now?"

Mr Fitzwarren seemed to think that Dick was.

"Dick," he said one day. "I need you and your cat to move into my warehouse. You must write down everything that comes and goes and keep a record of it.

"And Puss can catch the rats that have been gnawing my fine fabrics."

So Dick moved his bundle of belongings to the warehouse by the river. Ships came and ships went. Dick kept a record of it all.

"We're quite grand now, aren't we Puss?" he said.

But suddenly things changed. Somebody arrived who knew that Dick wasn't grand at all.

The squire's son arrived to be Mr Fitzwarren's new apprentice. He wasn't pleased to find Dick already there.

"Dick is really just a pig boy," he told the other apprentices. He made piggy faces to make the other boys laugh.

"I am not!" said Dick.

He took a step towards the squire's son. The squire's son stepped back and tripped – splat – into the smelly river mud! Then the other boys laughed at the squire's son.

"Pigs like rolling in mud!" they said, as they pointed and jeered at the squire's son.

The squire's son shouted at Dick, "I'll get you back for this, Pig Boy!"

Chapter 5

A Venture

Next day, Mr Fitzwarren's finest ship was due to sail.

"My ship, *The Unicorn*, is to go on a long voyage," he told everyone in his house. "She will sail to new places in search of new things to buy and sell. The Captain may find great treasure – or he may return home with nothing. He might even sink at sea."

Mr Fitzwarren continued, "Now, would any of you boys like to share in this big adventure? If you give something small to the Captain, he will try to trade it for you."

"Why don't you send something?" Alice asked Dick.

"I have nothing to send," he told her.

The squire's son knew how much Dick loved Puss.

"Every ship needs a cat, Pig Boy," he grinned.

"I've told you before," said Dick. "Puss is not for sale."

But after Dick had watched the ship slide slowly down the river to the sea, he couldn't find Puss anywhere.

"Puss!" Dick called in the warehouse.

"Puss!" he shouted along the riverside.

Puss didn't come. But the squire's son did.

"Your cat's on the ship," said the squire's son. "My friends gave her to the Captain for you, Pig Boy!"

"You stole Puss!"

Dick jumped at the squire's son.

They fought hard, wrestling and punching, but Dick won. Then he went back to the warehouse on his own and Mr Fitzwarren found him there.

"Is it true that you hit the squire's son, Dick Whittington?" asked Mr Fitzwarren. His face was red with anger.

"Yes," said Dick. "But only because…"

"There is no excuse for that sort of behaviour!" said Mr Fitzwarren.

Dick was ashamed. He had let down the man who had given him a job and a home.

Dick was lonely, too, without Puss.

"I can't ever become a gentleman now," he thought. "I'd best go back to being a pig boy for my old master, the farmer."

Chapter 6

Turn Again

Dick packed his bundle and put it on to his stick. He swung the stick over his shoulder and ran through the streets and out of London.

He didn't stop until he was in open fields.

Then Dick looked down on London and listened to the church bells, just as he had when he first arrived all those months before.

But this time, Dick knew where the bells were ringing from.

The bells from Bow Church seemed to be calling to him. Words came into Dick's head to fit their tune:

Turn again Whittington
Thou worthy citizen
Lord Mayor of London!

"That's true!" thought Dick. "I may not be rich. I may not always be good, but I am as worthy a citizen as anyone!"

He remembered how Puss hadn't given up when the big rat attacked her. "And neither will I," thought Dick.

And the bells agreed:

Turn again Whittington
Thou worthy citizen
Lord Mayor of London.

So Dick swung his bundle on to his back and headed back to London and the warehouse.

Chapter 7

Pearls and Kittens

Months passed before Dick heard anything about *The Unicorn*. The ship was waiting for the tide to bring her up the river to London.

"Please let Puss be safe on board!" thought Dick.

A crowd gathered to see the ship arrive. Dick helped unload the bundles and trunks and baskets of goods.

"Please, have you seen my cat?" he asked again and again. But no one had time to think about cats.

That evening, there was a feast at Mr Fitzwarren's house. Everyone was invited, even Dick.

Mr Fitzwarren told his apprentice boys, "There is something for each one of you in return for the goods that you sent on the voyage."

Dick watched as one by one the boys went up to get money and praise from the Captain. Last of all, the Captain called Dick.

"I have a story for you, young Dick," he said.

The Captain told a tale of a faraway land on the Barbary Coast of Africa.

He told of a grand king who gave a feast that was spoiled by rats.

"The rats stole all the food and there wasn't a cat in the place to sort them out," said the Captain.

"So I sent for Puss. She soon dealt with the rats, as you can imagine. None better! Then the king of that place said that he wanted Puss to catch all the rats in the kingdom."

Dick's hands clenched into fists.

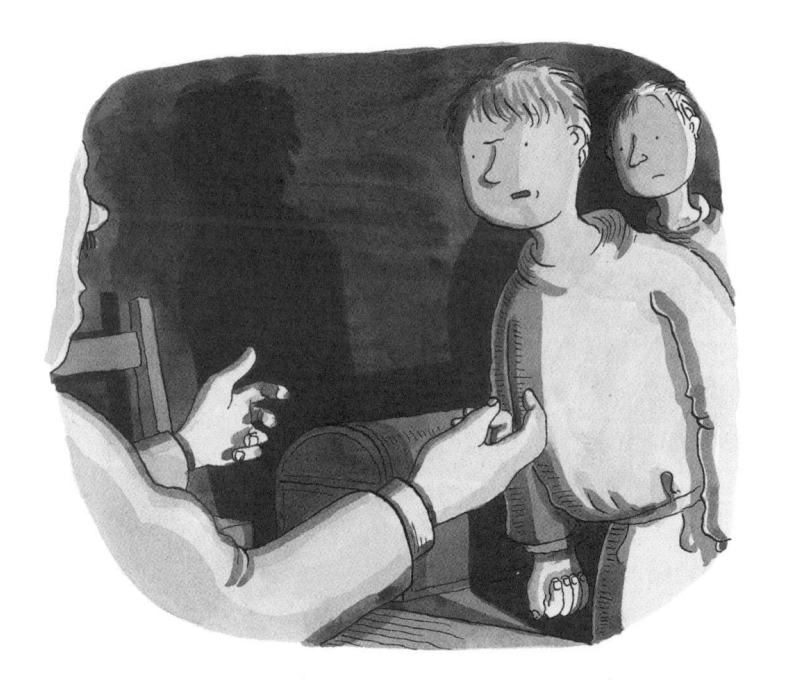

But the Captain went on, "Look in that chest, Dick. There's your reward from the King."

Slowly, Dick lifted the lid off the chest. Then he stared in wonder at piles of pearls and topazes, emeralds and diamonds, gold and spices and silks that lay within.

"What do you think of that, then?" asked the Captain.

Dick shook his head. However much treasure lay in that chest, he would still rather have Puss back.

The Captain smiled. "I didn't sell Puss," he said. "I sold her three kittens to the king."

"Kittens?" asked Dick.

The Captain laughed. "Your Puss grew plump on board ship and it wasn't from the mice and rats that she was catching."

The Captain continued, "One sunny evening in the southern seas, Puss settled on my bunk. When I went to bed, I found four fine kittens nestling at Puss's side!

"So, Dick, you have your cat back and you have treasure to make you a gentleman. That's the neatest bit of trading I've seen in all my years! I think that Mr Fitzwarren would agree."

"Yes, well done, Dick," said Mr Fitzwarren.

"Please, sir," said Dick. "Where is Puss now?"

Mr Fitzwarren pointed to Alice's room. "In there," he said.

Chapter 8

A Merchant Gentleman

Dick pushed the door and saw Puss, purring beside Alice.

Puss rose up on her toes and stretched and seemed to smile. She strode slowly across to Dick to rub against his legs.

"Puss!" laughed Dick, and he picked her up and cuddled her.

"And here's her handsome son," said Alice. She held up a kitten the colour of gold.

Dick gave the golden kitten to Alice. He sold the treasure. Then he paid to become Mr Fitzwarren's new apprentice.

In the years to come, Dick became a merchant with apprentices of his own. And ships, too. And a comfortable home.

Dick and Alice married. Master Dick Whittington was made Lord Mayor of London three times over.

He wore red and gold and the crowds cheered for him.

So his dream did come true.

And who do you think told all who would listen that Master Whittington had been his friend since they were boys together?

It was the squire's son, grown plump and bald and kind.

He would boast how he had known that grand man Dick Whittington, from the time they both lived in the same village.

And Dick would put an arm around the squire's son and say, "I wouldn't have all that I do now, if it wasn't for you."

Which was true, when you think about it.

But Dick never forgot where he had come from.

Every Christmas he sent fine cloth to his old master, the farmer, and his wife.

from Dick

He would sometimes visit old Cook
in her kitchen. He let her scold him
for not behaving like a gentleman
when he sat and peeled the potatoes and
listened to her grumbles.

Dick spent his money on hospitals and
libraries, churches and schools
for the poor of London. He gave them
clean water and had drains made
to take away the smelly filth.

And at the end of each day, Dick would sit with a cat on his lap and he would listen to the evening bells.

"Listen, Puss," he would say. "Can you pick out Bow Bells from that jangle?"

And one of Puss's children's children would open an eye and twitch her ears and hear:

Turn again, Whittington
Thou worthy citizen
Lord Mayor of London.

Then she would purr happily. And Dick Whittington would feel like purring, too.

About the author

I've always loved the story of Dick Whittington as a pantomime at Christmas – except for one thing. I don't like Dick selling his good friend, the cat, in exchange for his fortune. So I've put that right in my version of the story!

There was a real Richard Whittington who became Lord Mayor of London three times, almost seven hundred years ago. He didn't start life as a poor pig boy and may not even have had a cat. But stories don't have to be true to be good!